T0381378

Nana Jackie

presents

Jacquelyn Cauthen

To order additional copies of this book, contact:
Xlibris
844-714-8691
www.Xlibris.com
Orders@Xlibris.com

Illustrations by Jacquelyn Cauthen aka Nana Jackie
397 Charles St, Bridgeport Ct 06606
Nana Jackie portrait 'My Mother' drawn by Tarik Hamer ~ age 8
Bright Stars Poem writtenby Sean Hamer ~ age 9
www.SageJackiePoetry.com
email: sagegarden@acninc.net

ISBN: Softcover   978-1-4500-6481-1
          EBook   978-1-5434-9991-9

Print information available on the last page

Rev. date: 09/22/2021

MORNING GLORY LANE

Illustrated By:

JACQUELYN CAUTHEN

ONOMATOPEIA

BRIGHT STARS
PLANETARIUM

SNAP

MEOW

CRACKLE

ZING ZAP ZOOM BOOM

SLIDE

WATER

FOLLOW YOUR
HEART TOWER

THING-A-MA-JIC
TUNNEL

Introduction

The poems shared here are those I have named "Morning Glory Lane" poems. They reflect the recollections I have of children from my past to the children of my present. These poems come from exchanges which reflect sensitive, honest, humorous, loving, and real conversations. They were born in my communications and what I refer to as 'Sage Garden' experiences with children of all ages: inspired and written in their voices. What a pleasure and privilege! It's like a journey into our children's playgrounds where, as **Nana Jackie,** I get to enter and play in their "gardens" and nourish their "roots". There are no weeds here, only 'Morning Glories —enter *"How To Be A Poet"*.

In a time when so many of our children face all kinds of literacy challenges, the question arises of how to motivate your child when they won't read a book. My answer: use "literacy through poetry" exercises or programs where there is no right or wrong, test or contest , and your child's true potential, creativity and imagination can be discovered, encouraged and presented. Every child is a star —enter *"Bright Stars"*.

My mother was a wonderful southern woman who had barely finished grade school but had become a passionate reader. She understood that reading would open my mind to endless possibilities of what I could do and be. She taught me to read without the use of "phonics", DVD programs or having a "formal education". I can still remember the time she told me a story about her first parent- teacher meeting. After telling my mother that I had very good personal habits, agreeable social habits, "was a joy to others" and excellent work habits, the teacher asked her if she knew that I was an excellent reader. Momma just smiled and said "yes". That was my Kindergarten teacher, who really knew little about me, my life or my mother for that matter. My mother was my first and most important teacher. As a young child she told me that I was very smart and 'beautiful'. One day she showed me a picture book with a colored angel "just like me" I thought—enter *"Chocolate Face~ A Poem For Devon"*.

As soon as I could write my name, and met the age requirements, I registered and received a library card. I was in reader's wonderland. Going to the library was one of my favorite things and poetry brought a special joy. We didn't own a television until I was ten years old, and going to the movies or listening to the radio was a treat and a privilege. Neither my mother nor my father needed outside prompters or ratings like "parental discretion advised" or "PG ratings" to guide them in choosing or censoring what I would read or watch. I read novels, novelettes, and books with lots of short stories and poetry. There were the short poems that sometimes rhymed and others that did not. I also enjoyed the long poems that often told stories. I began my collection of writings and then wrote my own stories, created poetry books and kept a journal or diary. Although I did not save many of these journals in print, they were recorded in my mind and lived there alongside all the people, places and things I met in these books. Some people lived forever, others died and went to people heaven —enter *"Annibal's Best Friend Sharon"*.

All this reading led me to question everything and everyone. Family and friends described me as being "apt", and praised me for a vocabulary and knowledge well beyond my years. My father who was also an avid reader and collector of books, insisted on establishing a home library. Books were everywhere and both my parents passed onto me their love of reading. I developed a love of reading for all kinds of books. This passion included books from the writers of the great Harlem Renaissance to the authors of the "classics" and required school readings. My father gave me one other thing; his passion for numbers and Mathematics— enter *"Math Rules~ A Poem For Kadeem"*.

Lastly, as I mentioned earlier, somewhere between the age of five and six, my mother taught me to read. She was a Sunday school teacher and often read from her Holy Book. By the age of ten I would attend summer sleep-away camps sponsored by NYC Mission Society. I was a city girl learning to appreciate nature, wildflowers, trees, birds and bees: all God's creatures. It where I climbed 'Bald Mountain' and saw my first rainbow —enter *"Our Lady of Grace and The Children of The Rainbow"*.

There is love and hope, faith and grace, gladness and sadness, order and numbers, vibrant colors and beauty all around us. Enjoy your stay in Morning Glory Lane.

Yours from The Sage Garden
Jacquelyn 'Nana Jackie' Cauthen

Dedication

For my grandchildren Sekou Mosi, Jelani Naim,

Amber Corrina and Nala Keomi,

and to special family children, Aundre Lacy,

Layla Jo and Jasmine Brianna,

To all the children who have invited me to enter their

world, to share their journey and

inspired me to use their words and stories,

to be passed on.

Thank You, **Nana Jackie**

~~ SAGE GARDEN POEMS IN ~~

MORNING GLORY LANE

HOW TO BE A POET

CHOCOLATE FACE~A POEM FOR DEVON

BRIGHT STARS by Sean Hamer

ANNIBAL'S BESTFRIEND SHARON

MATH RULES A POEM FOR KADEEM

OUR LADY OF GRACE AND THE CHILDREN

OF THE RAINBOW

HOW TO BE A POET

Use your words.
All of them.
Sometimes even make up one.
It's Funtasticl

Read... Read... Read...
Read other people's poems.
Learn poetic rules from A to Z.
Then blend in serendipity. Be quiet.

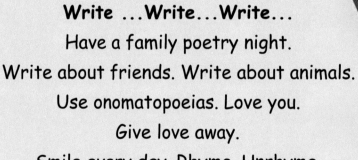

Write ...Write...Write...
Have a family poetry night.
Write about friends. Write about animals.
Use onomatopoeias. Love you.
Give love away.
Smile every day. Rhyme. Unrhyme.

Draw...Doodle...Scribble...
Giggle. Illustrate yourself. Pencil on.
Show off. Laugh whenever you want to.

Think... Think... Think...
Think details. Think Fun.
It's all right to be silly.
Hug idioms and puns.
Hola! Say how you feel. Adiosl
Feel what you say. Go fishing. Play.

Create...Create. .. Create...
Create what-ya-ma-call-its.
Make thing-a-ma-jigs. Do it now.

Don't forget the five senses.
Smell a Morning Glory.
Walk among the raindrops. Taste one.
Touch something fluffy. Sing a song.
Listen to the Sunrise.
Look for the Rainbow.

Follow Your Heart.

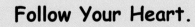

CHOCOLATE FACE

A POEM FOR DEVON

Devon went to school that day
To learn some stuff
but mostly play
Then out of the blue
everyone heard
well she was no lady
using those words
He thunk to himself-hummfl
She got some nerve
she got no shame
calling him right
out of his name

"CHOCOLATE FACE"

All of a sudden his

smile felt disgraced

His heart started pumpin'

like it does when you race

Someone just ought to

put her- in her place!

It was on--totally on
by now Devon just
REALLY wanted to
punch her lights out
you could see it in his eyes
there was no room for doubt
So he balled up his hand
to make a tight fist
And gave his best punch
Thank goodness –
He Missed

THAT'S WHEN
THE OLD LADY
CARRIED HIM
RIGHT OUT
Of the classroom
and he
didn't even get
a chance ~
to tell her
his name
was not

CHOCOLATE FACE

PRINCIPAL

Devon thought to himself
It's just not fair
She started it all
Doesn't anyone care
Just at that moment
Nursey Jack came along
She seemed to be nice
A friendship might form
"Que pasa mi amigo?"
She asked-he replied
Told her his story
And then-to his surprise
She smiled and hugged him
With her very
Best hug and said-
Don't you know
It's chocolate I love
I love chocolate things
Chocolate people and
Chocolate places
So naturally I love-all chocolate Faces

CHOCOLATE IS
MY MOST FAVORITE THING!

Then Devon remembered
He loved chocolate too
He began to feel better
Good things-
This was true
Like... hot cocoa
In the winter
Everyone likes hot chocolate!!
Chocolate Easter Bunnies
In the spring-Ring Dings!!
Like...chewy, crunchy dark
Chocolate-Chunkies!!

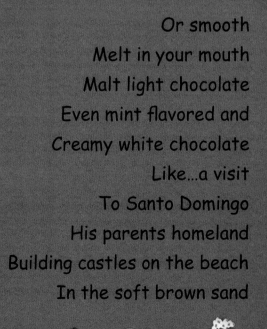

Or smooth
Melt in your mouth
Malt light chocolate
Even mint flavored and
Creamy white chocolate
Like...a visit
To Santo Domingo
His parents homeland
Building castles on the beach
In the soft brown sand

Playing in the hot hot Sun
It's how he got the tan
THAT'S WHY HE WAS CHOCOLATE BROWN!

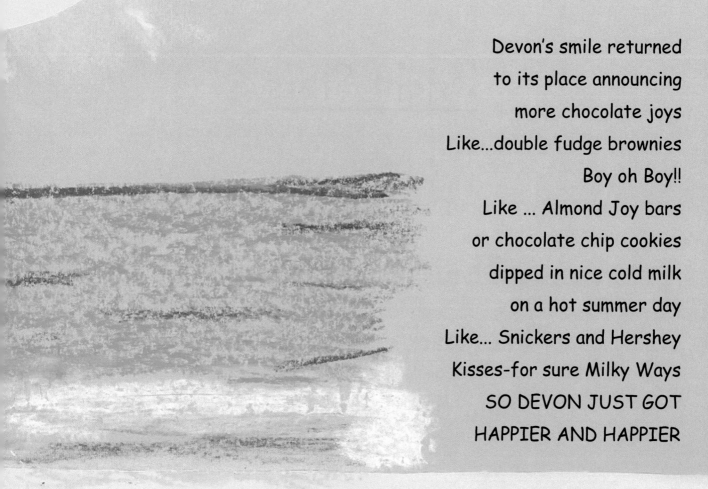

Devon's smile returned
to its place announcing
more chocolate joys
Like...double fudge brownies
Boy oh Boy!!
Like ... Almond Joy bars
or chocolate chip cookies
dipped in nice cold milk
on a hot summer day
Like... Snickers and Hershey
Kisses-for sure Milky Ways
SO DEVON JUST GOT
HAPPIER AND HAPPIER

'cause he knew everybody
likes Chocolate and if
that's the case
It's really not a bad thing
if someone calls you
CHOCOLATE FACE
Devon went to school that day
To learn some stuff-
But mostly play

Bright Stars

Bright Stars

They light at night

They sparkle when its dark

They light so much you

Can see them

Dippers

By SEAN

ANNIBAL'S BEST FRIEND SHARON

She made him laugh
until he cried-
By the things she did
My oh my!!
Squealin',rollin'
Bumpin and thumpin'
Crawlin',runnin'
sometimes jumpin'!
They shared a
very special joy
He was just
a gentle boy
and she
a little baby
Hamster when
first they met

Annibal knew
Sharon was much
more than his pet

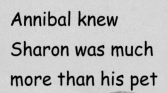

Sharon taught Annibal
all one should know
About the nature
of living things
Big and small
He learned the
language of Animals
And taught her
the language of people

DOCTOR DOOLITTLE
MEET
DOCTOR ANNIBAL

They talked
and played
And played
and talked

For days on end
Sharon was
Annibal's best friend

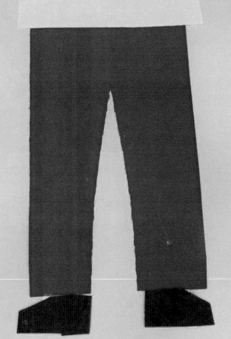

Annibal was always
kind-hearted
he was never
ever mean
he groomed
her daily
and kept her
squeaky clean
Even when Sharon
was four years old
Her fur was fluffy
like a ball of cotton
Black cotton
on the bottom
light reddish-brown
on the top
with snow white
patches on her face

He made her
a Hamster home
And called it **Sharon's Place**

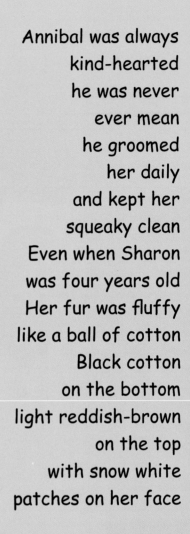

Sharon had two
cheek pouches
in which
she stuffed
extra food
And fed herself
where ever and
whenever she felt
in the mood and
Annibal gave her
the best to eat
sharing with her
his special treats
Once She was
fully grown
They vowed
to never part

Sharon could still fit
in Annibal 's pocket
The one right over his heart

It really was
the saddest day
when he found out
She died...
He·just
Cried and cried
and cried
He was heartbroken..
Still he understood
That we cannot
Always choose
What or when
Or who we lose

Annibal had learned
A lesson on
Living and dying
The funeral was on
A bright sunny day
Sharon's time had
Come to rest

In Hamster Heaven
Annibal was
just eleven

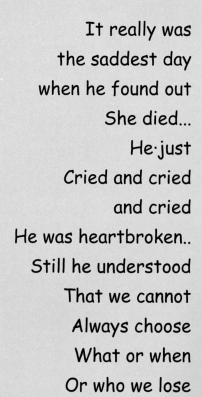

MATH RULES!!
APOEM FOR KADEEM

Kadeem was cool 'cause
He already learned the basic math rules

On his last birthday he was 3X3 years old
Quite the scholar and math wizard I'm told
After all- there were only 10 digits

Playing with numbers was easy-it's true
Like subtraction, division, the times tables too
Plus- clever addition game clues

He liked school and being in the 2+2 grade
Nurse Jackie said "guess what"
These rules never change

He could multiply most anything in his mind
Like 3x3 =9 and 3x9 =27 and
and 3x27 =81- even 3x243 =729 !!

Some said one day he would be
the **Greatest** somebody a
MATHEMATICIAN

Or Astronaut or Physician or
Commander-in-Chief or
Magician or **King of the World**

But first he would have to
-you know- grow up

26

Kadeem was cool 'cause
He already knew for sure- **Math Rules!!**

OUR LADY OF GRACE AND
THE CHILDREN OF THE RAINBOW

She was called
Our Lady of Grace
The Holy name given to
their school building place

Her picture adorning
the vestibule wall
A blessing and welcome
to one and to all

She brought them
glad tidings and joy
Sunbeams
of **GRACE**
and showers
of
FAITH

Everyone was
excited
Their hearts
were delighted
-that special day
grades one to eight
and of course Pre-k!

They had
to hurry-
they had to
make haste- down
the hall-up the stairs
to the healing room space
"Let's go" said the elder
There was no time to waste

Baby brown sugar'
Angels called it
Nurse
Jackie's Place
of course
it was she
who in fact
led the race

30

Thunder Lords boomed
out their goodbye
While crystal raindrops
hoped and sighed
Gray cottony clouds
moseyed on by

Some claimed
to have never
seen such a
view

As Mother Nature
served her
wondrous hues

31

Our Lady of Grace
smiled on nigh
Beautiful rainbow
embraced blue sky
Creation of
The One Most High

As they
watched
two-by-two
A Mother's
voice
whispered
I love each of you'

33

How To Be A Poet

How to motivate your child to succeed in school when they won't read a book

Use "Literacy Through Poetry" to discover your child's true

Potential,

Creativity, and

Imagination

Nana Jackie
Presents
Sage Garden Poetry"
Edutainment DVD

Poems & Illustrations by
Jacquelyn Cauthen

To order contact:
JACQUELYN CAUTHEN
www.SageJackiePoetry.com

A Note From Nana Jackie
Literacy through Poetry Workbook

I am often invited by school groups,
community and church youth groups,
friends and family to share my poems,
I love presenting to children of all ages.

In response to these invitations,
and now that I am a grandmother and
"village elder", I see the ongoing
need for these 'live' presentations.
Here the children get to witness,
the art of poetry.

Since I can only be in one place
at one time I have designed a creative
"Things to Do" work book with.
activities for each poem in this set.

MY MOTHER By Tarik Hamer, age 8

For more things to do, I have written and produced an edutainment video inviting active participation. .Here children see, hear, and read along. There are no flashing lights, bells or whistles or bouncing balls here. This video presentation is a live recording, made for, by and of actual school age children. There are many additional poems to enjoy and more Sage Garden Poetry books are on the "artist easel". The Morning Glory Lane collection is Book I.

*Meanwhile, I encourage everyone to join in my poetry program, **parents** and grandparents childcare givers and teachers, to become poetically playful:…. revisit childhood memories…. assist the children everywhere… review all the activities sheets and DVD … and of course— come poet with me.*

Yours from the Sage Garden
Nana Jackie

NANA JACKIE'S HIDDEN CLUE

Find all 20 words below in the maze to reveal a hidden clue

```
E E C H O C O L D R A T
E T F A C E P R D A T O
W S I M O H A E K I O T
E A S R E W O L F N U E
S T I U W T D G W B C O
D N E I R F U G W O H P
S L A M I N A I D W S Y
W A T H I N K G G A X K
M D Q M E S M I L E E S
S I H U G A S M E L L R
S O K L A W R A L O H C
K S G P L I S T E N K D
```

ADIOS	ANIMALS	DRAW	FLOWERS
FRIEND	GIGGLE	HEART	HOLA
HUG	LISTEN	POET	RAINBOW
READ	SMELLL	SMILE	TASTE
THINK	TOUCH	WALK	WRITE

_ _ _ _ _ _ _ _ _   _ _ _ _

THINGS TO DO: INSIDE MORNING GLORY LANE

TO BE A POET ....Play with words and phrases.
Write and read all kinds of poetry.

CHOCOLATE FACE   Draw or paint a picture of your favorite
A POEM FOR DEVON...................person, place, thing,
Complete the hidden clue puzzle

BRIGHT STARS............................Look towards the sky on a clear night
then draw what you see or imagine .
Go to the Planetarium and learn when
And where to look for Zodiac stars

ANNIBAL'S BEST FRIEND.........If you have a pet or know someone with
SHARON   a pet:-- learn about animals that you can
care for and that make good pets

MATH RULES!!   Learn the basic math rules.
\POEM FOR K ADEEM ....Numbers are everywhere and in
everything; Look up pantomimes

OUR LADY OF GRACE and   Write a poem about the special
THE CHILDREN   events or things or creations occurring in nature
THE RAINBOW ....Draw or paint a picture that has a
Rainbow in it.

NANA JACKIE Presents   View Nana Jackie on her DVD
Sage Garden Poetry ....Watch, listen, and read along with
Actual Presentation

For more info contact: sagegarden@acninc.net att: Nana Jackie Poems

MORE THINGS TO DO :
AT HOME or IN THE NEIGHBORHOOD

Favorite Poem Project: Have a weekly or monthly family poetry reading right in your home. Ask parents, grandparents, neighbors to share their favorite poem. Each participant reads their favorite poem and says why they wrote it or why they like it. Form teams and have everyone contribute lines to create a poem

Where to go: Take a trip to the library or local bookstore where there are free scheduled poetry readings. Meet the poet and listen to the "voice" of poet; how they express themselves and share their poems. Check your local newspaper for other community poetry events. Many poets are also story tellers.

"Poetry Slam": You can start a family, friends or school or poetry club-tell everyone. Next, have a competition/contest where the poets get up in front of an audience. This is an exciting event where poets "show off" their words and their different styles. Everyone is involved, by either performing or judging the Poetry.

Time Out: Everyone needs a quiet time. Mom, Dad, sister, brother, and **YOU**. It's always good to find a quiet private place where you can just read and write. Family members can agree to a scheduled block of time where a designated area is only to be used for reading or writing poetry.

READ…READ…READ for enjoyment 10 minutes EVERY DAY: Whenever possible buy one book a month and START YOUR OWN LIBRARY. This way you can to re-read your favorite book or maybe trade books with good friends.

QUICK-TIP LESSONS # 1- 7:

TRANSFORMING WORDS INTO ART: The following tips can be applied to any poetry and of course applied those in Morning Glory Lane.
Writing poetry is a personal, unique and wonderfully satisfying experience.

Lesson #1; The <u>Theme-</u> What was the poem about? What's the big idea ? This is the point the writer is trying to make about a subject.

Lesson #2: The <u>Purpose</u> Did you learn anything from the poem? This is where you find out what can be learned

Lesson #3: The <u>Mood</u> –How did the poem make you feel?
How do you feel about the theme? Is it silly, serious, funny, sad, exciting?

Lesson #4: The <u>Form</u> - Did you like the way the poem was put together? why? This could be structured and rule oriented or free style.

Lesson #5: Rhythm and Rhyme.
Rhythm: a poetic form where poets read and speak their poem
with a unique beat or cadence. Rhyming: using words that sound alike.
'Spoken Word Artist' often do both and sometimes use background music

Lesson #6: Onomatopoeias. Some poems use the imitation of natural sounds in word form, for example Zap/Hiss/Boom/Moo/Buzz" These are often found in comic strips, and comic books, and cartoons
Lesson #7. The Art in Poetry: Pictures and illustrations can bring more life to your poetry. You can also use collage, mobile, computer graphics, rubbings, and cartooning. Make a basic Artbox with crayons, colored pencils, markers and paints That's what I did—You Can Too!

40

WHAT-YA-MA-CALL-IT
BALLOONS

41

Printed in the United States
by Baker & Taylor Publisher Services